YO-CBT-889

BLESS THE DAY

365 Verses from the BIBLE

IDEALS PUBLICATIONS INCORPORATED
NASHVILLE, TENNESSEE

Designed by Peggy Murphy-Jones

Published by Ideals Publications Incorporated
535 Metroplex Drive, Suite 250
Nashville, Tennessee 37211

ISBN 0-8249-5833-0

10 8 6 4 2 1 3 5 7 9

∂ CONTENTS ৯

JANUARY 1
Blessed are the poor in spirit: for theirs is the kingdom of heaven. – *Matthew 5:3*

JANUARY 2
And the LORD God formed man of the dust of the ground, and breathed into his nostrils the breath of life; and man became a living soul.
– *Genesis 2:7*

JANUARY 3
To every thing there is a season, and a time to every purpose under the heaven.
– *Ecclesiastes 3:1*

JANUARY 4
He hath made every thing beautiful in his time: also he hath set the world in their heart, so that no man can find out the work that God maketh from the beginning to the end.
– *Ecclesiastes 3:11*

JANUARY 5
Make a joyful noise unto the LORD, all ye lands.
– *Psalm 100:1*

JANUARY 6
Serve the LORD with gladness: come before his presence with singing. – *Psalm 100:2*

JANUARY 7
Enter into his gates with thanksgiving, and into his courts with praise: be thankful unto him, and bless his name. – *Psalm 100:4*

JANUARY 8
Know ye that the LORD he is God: it is he that hath made us, and not we ourselves; we are his people, and the sheep of his pasture.
– *Psalm 100:3*

JANUARY 9
For the LORD is good; his mercy is everlasting; and his truth endureth to all generations.
– *Psalm 100:5*

JANUARY 10
O LORD our Lord, how excellent is thy name in all the earth! who hast set thy glory above the heavens. – *Psalm 8:1*

JANUARY 11
When I consider thy heavens, the work of thy fingers, the moon and the stars, which thou hast ordained; What is man, that thou art mindful of him? and the son of man, that thou visitest him? – *Psalm 8:3-4*

JANUARY 12
I am the LORD, and there is none else, there is no God beside me. – *Isaiah 45:5a*

JANUARY 13
O LORD our Lord, how excellent is thy name in all the earth! – *Psalm 8:9*

JANUARY 14
Sing unto the LORD; for he hath done excellent things: this is known in all the earth.
– *Isaiah 12:5*

JANUARY 15
I delight to do thy will, O my God: yea, thy law is within my heart. – *Psalm 40:8*

JANUARY 16
I was glad when they said unto me, Let us go into the house of the LORD. – *Psalm 122:1*

JANUARY 17
This is the day which the LORD hath made; we will rejoice and be glad in it.
– *Psalm 118:24*

JANUARY 18
For ye shall go out with joy, and be led forth with peace: the mountains and the hills shall break forth before you into singing, and all the trees of the field shall clap their hands.
– *Isaiah 55:12*

JANUARY 19
O LORD, thou art my God; I will exalt thee, I will praise thy name; for thou hast done wonderful things; thy counsels of old are faithfulness and truth. – *Isaiah 25:1*

JANUARY 20
LORD, thou hast been our dwelling place in all generations. – *Psalm 90:1*

JANUARY 21
Arise, shine; for thy light is come, and the glory of the LORD is risen upon thee.
– *Isaiah 60:1*

JANUARY 22
Therefore with joy shall ye draw water out of the wells of salvation. – *Isaiah 12:3*

JANUARY 23
And in that day shall ye say, Praise the LORD, call upon his name, declare his doings among the people, make mention that his name is exalted. – *Isaiah 12:4*

JANUARY 24
Sing unto the LORD; for he hath done excellent things: this is known in all the earth. – *Isaiah 12:5*

JANUARY 25
Sing praises to God, sing praises: sing praises unto our King, sing praises. – *Psalm 47:6*

JANUARY 26
Before the mountains were brought forth, or ever thou hadst formed the earth and the world, even from everlasting to everlasting, thou art God. – *Psalm 90:2*

JANUARY 27
And Mary said, My soul doth magnify the Lord, And my spirit hath rejoiced in God my Saviour. – *Luke 1:46-47*

JANUARY 28
Sing unto the LORD a new song, and his praise from the end of the earth. – *Isaiah 42:10a*

JANUARY 29
And he hath put a new song in my mouth, even praise unto our God: many shall see it, and fear, and shall trust in the LORD.
– *Psalm 40:3*

JANUARY 30
O sing unto the LORD a new song: sing unto the LORD, all the earth. – *Psalm 96:1*

JANUARY 31
Sing unto the LORD, bless his name; shew forth his salvation from day to day.
– *Psalm 96:2*

FEBRUARY 1
Declare his glory among the heathen, his wonders among all people. – *Psalm 96:3*

FEBRUARY 2
For the LORD is great, and greatly to be praised: he is to be feared above all gods.
– *Psalm 96:4*

FEBRUARY 3
Rejoice in the Lord alway: and again I say, Rejoice. – *Philippians 4:4*

FEBRUARY 4
The heavens declare the glory of God; and the firmament sheweth his handywork.
– *Psalm 19:1*

FEBRUARY 5
Therefore will I offer in his tabernacle sacrifices of joy; I will sing, yea, I will sing praises unto the LORD. – *Psalm 27:6b*

FEBRUARY 6
Let not your heart be troubled: ye believe in God, believe also in me. – *John 14:1*

FEBRUARY 7
In my Father's house are many mansions: if it were not so, I would have told you. I go to prepare a place for you. – *John 14:2*

FEBRUARY 8
And if I go and prepare a place for you, I will come again, and receive you unto myself; that where I am, there ye may be also. – *John 14:3*

FEBRUARY 9
The LORD is my shepherd; I shall not want.
– *Psalm 23:1*

FEBRUARY 10
Yea, though I walk through the valley of the shadow of death, I will fear no evil: for thou art with me; thy rod and thy staff they comfort me. – *Psalm 23:4*

FEBRUARY 11
And there are diversities of operations, but it is the same God which worketh all in all.
– *1 Corinthians 12:6*

FEBRUARY 12
I will lift up mine eyes unto the hills, from whence cometh my help. – *Psalm 121:1*

FEBRUARY 13
My help cometh from the LORD, which made heaven and earth. – *Psalm 121:2*

FEBRUARY 14
Incline your ear, and come unto me: hear, and your soul shall live; and I will make an everlasting covenant with you, even the sure mercies of David. – *Isaiah 55:3*

FEBRUARY 15
He shall feed his flock like a shepherd: he shall gather the lambs with his arm, and carry them in his bosom, and shall gently lead those that are with young. – *Isaiah 40:11*

FEBRUARY 16
O God, thou art my God; early will I seek thee: my soul thirsteth for thee, my flesh longeth for thee in a dry and thirsty land, where no water is. – *Psalm 63:1*

FEBRUARY 17
Comfort ye, comfort ye my people, saith your God. – *Isaiah 40:1*

FEBRUARY 18
My sheep hear my voice, and I know them, and they follow me. – *John 10:27*

FEBRUARY 19
And I give unto them eternal life; and they shall never perish, neither shall any man pluck them out of my hand. – *John 10:28*

FEBRUARY 20
My Father, which gave them me, is greater than all; and no man is able to pluck them out of my Father's hand. – *John 10:29*

FEBRUARY 21
And whither I go ye know, and the way ye know. – *John 14:4*

FEBRUARY 22
Come unto me, all ye that labour and are heavy laden, and I will give you rest.
– *Matthew 11:28*

FEBRUARY 23
Take my yoke upon you, and learn of me; for I am meek and lowly in heart: and ye shall find rest unto your souls. – *Matthew 11:29*

FEBRUARY 24
For my yoke is easy, and my burden is light.
– *Matthew 11:30*

FEBRUARY 25
How think ye? if a man have an hundred sheep, and one of them be gone astray, doth he not leave the ninety and nine, and goeth into the mountains, and seeketh that which is gone astray? – *Matthew 18:12*

FEBRUARY 26
And if so be that he find it, verily I say unto you, he rejoiceth more of that sheep, than of the ninety and nine which went not astray.
– *Matthew 18:13*

FEBRUARY 27
I am the good shepherd, and know my sheep, and am known of mine. – *John 10:14*

FEBRUARY 28
As the Father knoweth me, even so know I the Father: and I lay down my life for the sheep. – *John 10:15*

MARCH 1
I will go before thee, and make the crooked places straight: I will break in pieces the gates of brass, and cut in sunder the bars of iron.
– *Isaiah 45:2*

MARCH 2
And I will give thee the treasures of darkness, and hidden riches of secret places, that thou mayest know that I, the LORD, which call thee by thy name, am the God of Israel.
– *Isaiah 45:3*

MARCH 3
But Jesus said, Suffer little children, and forbid them not, to come unto me: for of such is the kingdom of heaven. – *Matthew 19:14*

MARCH 4
I and my Father are one. – *John 10:30*

MARCH 5
For, behold, I create new heavens and a new earth: and the former shall not be remembered, nor come into mind. – *Isaiah 65:17*

MARCH 6
Blessed are they which are persecuted for righteousness' sake: for theirs is the kingdom of heaven. – *Matthew 5:10*

MARCH 7
Blessed are ye, when men shall revile you, and persecute you, and shall say all manner of evil against you falsely, for my sake.
– *Matthew 5:11*

MARCH 8
Rejoice, and be exceeding glad: for great is your reward in heaven: for so persecuted they the prophets which were before you.
– *Matthew 5:12*

MARCH 9
And I will pray the Father, and he shall give you another Comforter, that he may abide with you for ever. – *John 14:16*

MARCH 10
Even the Spirit of truth; whom the world cannot receive, because it seeth him not, neither knoweth him: but ye know him; for he dwelleth with you, and shall be in you.
– *John 14:17*

MARCH 11
I will not leave you comfortless: I will come to you. – *John 14:18*

MARCH 12
I can do all things through Christ which strengtheneth me. – *Philippians 4:13*

MARCH 13
And we know that all things work together for good to them that love God, to them who are the called according to his purpose.
– *Romans 8:28*

MARCH 14
What shall we then say to these things? If God be for us, who can be against us?
– *Romans 8:31*

MARCH 15
I have set the LORD always before me: because he is at my right hand, I shall not be moved. – *Psalm 16:8*

MARCH 16
Fear thou not; for I am with thee: be not dismayed; for I am thy God: I will strengthen thee; yea, I will help thee; yea, I will uphold thee with the right hand of my righteousness.
– *Isaiah 41:10*

MARCH 17
I will love thee, O LORD, my strength.
– *Psalm 18:1*

MARCH 18
And Jesus looking upon them saith, With men it is impossible, but not with God: for with God all things are possible. – *Mark 10:27*

MARCH 19
For I the LORD thy God will hold thy right hand, saying unto thee, Fear not; I will help thee. – *Isaiah 41:13*

MARCH 20
Behold, God is my salvation; I will trust, and not be afraid: for the LORD JEHOVAH is my strength and my song; he also is become my salvation. – *Isaiah 12:2*

MARCH 21
He giveth power to the faint; and to them that have no might he increaseth strength.
– *Isaiah 40:29*

MARCH 22
Be strong and of a good courage, fear not, nor be afraid of them: for the LORD thy God, he it is that doth go with thee; he will not fail thee, nor forsake thee. – *Deuteronomy 31:6*

MARCH 23
The LORD is my strength and my shield; my heart trusted in him, and I am helped: therefore my heart greatly rejoiceth; and with my song will I praise him. – *Psalm 28:7*

MARCH 24
The LORD is my light and my salvation; whom shall I fear? the LORD is the strength of my life; of whom shall I be afraid? – *Psalm 27:1*

MARCH 25
God is our refuge and strength, a very present help in trouble. – *Psalm 46:1*

MARCH 26
Therefore will not we fear, though the earth be removed, and though the mountains be carried into the midst of the sea. – *Psalm 46:2*

MARCH 27
But as he which hath called you is holy, so be ye holy in all manner of conversation.
– *1 Peter 1:15*

MARCH 28
The LORD is my rock, and my fortress, and my deliverer; my God, my strength, in whom I will trust; my buckler, and the horn of my salvation, and my high tower. – *Psalm 18:2*

MARCH 29
Hast thou not known? hast thou not heard, that the everlasting God, the LORD, the Creator of the ends of the earth, fainteth not, neither is weary? there is no searching of his understanding. – *Isaiah 40:28*

MARCH 30
And he said unto me, My grace is sufficient for thee: for my strength is made perfect in weakness. Most gladly therefore will I rather glory in my infirmities, that the power of Christ may rest upon me. – *2 Corinthians 12:9*

MARCH 31
Even the youths shall faint and be weary, and the young men shall utterly fall. – *Isaiah 40:30*

APRIL 1
But they that wait upon the LORD shall renew their strength; they shall mount up with wings as eagles; they shall run, and not be weary; and they shall walk, and not faint. – *Isaiah 40:31*

APRIL 2
Who shall stand in his holy place? He that hath clean hands, and a pure heart; who hath not lifted up his soul unto vanity, nor sworn deceitfully. – *Psalm 24:3b-4*

APRIL 3
Because it is written, Be ye holy; for I am holy. – *1 Peter 1:16*

APRIL 4
Then shall ye call upon me, and ye shall go and pray unto me, and I will hearken unto you. – *Jeremiah 29:12*

APRIL 5
And ye shall seek me, and find me, when ye shall search for me with all your heart.
– *Jeremiah 29:13*

APRIL 6
But he answered and said, It is written, Man shall not live by bread alone, but by every word that proceedeth out of the mouth of God. – *Matthew 4:4*

APRIL 7
He that loveth father or mother more than me is not worthy of me: and he that loveth son or daughter more than me is not worthy of me.
– *Matthew 10:37*

APRIL 8
Have not I commanded thee? Be strong and of a good courage; be not afraid, neither be thou dismayed: for the LORD thy God is with thee whithersoever thou goest. – *Joshua 1:9*

APRIL 9
For we wrestle not against flesh and blood, but against principalities, against powers, against the rulers of the darkness of this world, against spiritual wickedness in high places.
– *Ephesians 6:12*

APRIL 10
Ye are the light of the world. A city that is set on an hill cannot be hid. – *Matthew 5:14*

APRIL 11
Neither do men light a candle, and put it under a bushel, but on a candlestick; and it giveth light unto all that are in the house.
– *Matthew 5:15*

APRIL 12
Let your light so shine before men, that they may see your good works, and glorify your Father which is in heaven. – *Matthew 5:16*

APRIL 13
Then said Jesus to those Jews which believed on him, If ye continue in my word, then are ye my disciples indeed. – *John 8:31*

APRIL 14
And ye shall know the truth, and the truth shall make you free. – *John 8:32*

APRIL 15
Enter ye in at the strait gate: for wide is the gate, and broad is the way, that leadeth to destruction, and many there be which go in thereat. – *Matthew 7:13*

APRIL 16
Because strait is the gate, and narrow is the way, which leadeth unto life, and few there be that find it. – *Matthew 7:14*

APRIL 17
But be ye doers of the word, and not hearers only, deceiving your own selves. – *James 1:22*

APRIL 18
What? know ye not that your body is the temple of the Holy Ghost which is in you, which ye have of God, and ye are not your own?
– *1 Corinthians 6:19*

APRIL 19
For ye are bought with a price: therefore glorify God in your body, and in your spirit, which are God's. – *1 Corinthians 6:20*

APRIL 20
Draw nigh to God, and he will draw nigh to you. Cleanse your hands, ye sinners; and purify your hearts, ye double minded.
– *James 4:8*

APRIL 21
If any man among you seem to be religious, and bridleth not his tongue, but deceiveth his own heart, this man's religion is vain.
– *James 1:26*

APRIL 22
He maketh his sun to rise on the evil and on the good, and sendeth rain on the just and on the unjust. – *Matthew 5:45b*

APRIL 23
For if ye love them which love you, what reward have ye? do not even the publicans the same? – *Matthew 5:46*

APRIL 24
Pray without ceasing. – *1 Thessalonians 5:17*

APRIL 25
And if ye salute your brethren only, what do ye more than others? do not even the publicans so? – *Matthew 5:47*

APRIL 26
I beseech you therefore, brethren, by the mercies of God, that ye present your bodies a living sacrifice, holy, acceptable unto God, which is your reasonable service. – *Romans 12:1*

APRIL 27
And be not conformed to this world: but be ye transformed by the renewing of your mind, that ye may prove what is that good, and acceptable, and perfect, will of God.
– *Romans 12:2*

APRIL 28
Let love be without dissimulation. Abhor that which is evil; cleave to that which is good.
– *Romans 12:9*

APRIL 29
Be kindly affectioned one to another with brotherly love; in honour preferring one another; Not slothful in business; fervent in spirit; serving the Lord. – *Romans 12:10-11*

APRIL 30
And Jesus answered and said unto him, Get thee behind me, Satan: for it is written, Thou shalt worship the Lord thy God, and him only shalt thou serve. – *Luke 4:8*

MAY 1
Who can find a virtuous woman? for her price is far above rubies. – *Proverbs 31:10*

MAY 2
Strength and honour are her clothing; and she shall rejoice in time to come. – *Proverbs 31:25*

MAY 3
She openeth her mouth with wisdom; and in her tongue is the law of kindness.
– *Proverbs 31:26*

MAY 4
She looketh well to the ways of her household, and eateth not the bread of idleness.
– *Proverbs 31:27*

MAY 5
Her children arise up, and call her blessed; her husband also, and he praiseth her.
– *Proverbs 31:28*

MAY 6
Blessed is the man that walketh not in the counsel of the ungodly, nor standeth in the way of sinners, nor sitteth in the seat of the scornful. – *Psalm 1:1*

MAY 7
But his delight is in the law of the LORD; and in his law doth he meditate day and night.
– *Psalm 1:2*

MAY 8
As it is written, There is none righteous, no, not one. – *Romans 3:10*

MAY 9
There is none that understandeth, there is none that seeketh after God. – *Romans 3:11*

MAY 10
Heaven and earth shall pass away: but my words shall not pass away. – *Mark 13:31*

MAY 11
Be not deceived; God is not mocked: for what-soever a man soweth, that shall he also reap.
– *Galatians 6:7*

MAY 12
And if it seem evil unto you to serve the LORD, choose you this day whom ye will serve; whether the gods which your fathers served that were on the other side of the flood, or the gods of the Amorites, in whose land ye dwell: but as for me and my house, we will serve the LORD. – *Joshua 24:15*

MAY 13
Take heed that ye despise not one of these little ones; for I say unto you, That in heaven their angels do always behold the face of my Father which is in heaven. – *Matthew 18:10*

MAY 14
Quench not the Spirit. – *1 Thessalonians 5:19*

MAY 15
In every thing give thanks: for this is the will
of God in Christ Jesus concerning you.
– *1 Thessalonians 5:18*

MAY 16
Whosoever shall lose his life for my sake and
the gospel's, the same shall save it. – *Mark 8:35b*

MAY 17
Prove all things; hold fast that which is good.
– *1 Thessalonians 5:21*

MAY 18
Abstain from all appearance of evil.
– *1 Thessalonians 5:22*

MAY 19
And the very God of peace sanctify you
wholly; and I pray God your whole spirit and
soul and body be preserved blameless unto
the coming of our Lord Jesus Christ.
– *1 Thessalonians 5:23*

MAY 20
Faithful is he that calleth you, who also will do
it. – *1 Thessalonians 5:24*

MAY 21
Watch therefore: for ye know not what hour
your Lord doth come. – *Matthew 24:42*

MAY 22
Be ye therefore perfect, even as your Father
which is in heaven is perfect. – *Matthew 5:48*

MAY 23

His lord said unto him, Well done, thou good and faithful servant: thou hast been faithful over a few things, I will make thee ruler over many things: enter thou into the joy of thy lord. – *Matthew 25:21*

MAY 24

That all men should honour the Son, even as they honour the Father. He that honoureth not the Son honoureth not the Father which hath sent him. – *John 5:23*

MAY 25

And he said unto them, Go ye into all the world, and preach the gospel to every creature. – *Mark 16:15*

MAY 26

But the fruit of the Spirit is love, joy, peace, longsuffering, gentleness, goodness, faith, Meekness, temperance: against such there is no law. – *Galatians 5:22-23*

MAY 27

And they that are Christ's have crucified the flesh with the affections and lusts.
– *Galatians 5:24*

MAY 28

Now the God of patience and consolation grant you to be likeminded one toward another according to Christ Jesus.
– *Romans 15:5*

MAY 29

For he that soweth to his flesh shall of the flesh reap corruption; but he that soweth to the Spirit shall of the Spirit reap life everlasting. – *Galatians 6:8*

MAY 30

And let us not be weary in well doing: for in due season we shall reap, if we faint not.
– *Galatians 6:9*

MAY 31

Abide in me, and I in you. As the branch cannot bear fruit of itself, except it abide in the vine; no more can ye, except ye abide in me.
– *John 15:4*

JUNE 1

I am the vine, ye are the branches: He that abideth in me, and I in him, the same bringeth forth much fruit: for without me ye can do nothing. – *John 15:5*

JUNE 2

And if thy right hand offend thee, cut it off, and cast it from thee: for it is profitable for thee that one of thy members should perish, and not that thy whole body should be cast into hell. – *Matthew 5:30*

JUNE 3

And be ye kind one to another, tenderhearted, forgiving one another, even as God for Christ's sake hath forgiven you. – *Ephesians 4:32*

JUNE 4
Now ye are clean through the word which I have spoken unto you. – *John 15:3*

JUNE 5
And he saith unto them, Follow me, and I will make you fishers of men. – *Matthew 4:19*

JUNE 6
And they straightway left their nets, and followed him. – *Matthew 4:20*

JUNE 7
Then said Jesus to them again, Peace be unto you: as my Father hath sent me, even so send I you. – *John 20:21*

JUNE 8
A friend loveth at all times. – *Proverbs 17:17a*

JUNE 9
For whosoever shall call upon the name of the Lord shall be saved. – *Romans 10:13*

JUNE 10
But the Comforter, which is the Holy Ghost, whom the Father will send in my name, he shall teach you all things, and bring all things to your remembrance, whatsoever I have said unto you. – *John 14:26*

JUNE 11
If we live in the Spirit, let us also walk in the Spirit. – *Galatians 5:25*

JUNE 12

That ye may with one mind and one mouth glorify God, even the Father of our Lord Jesus Christ. – *Romans 15:6*

JUNE 13

Wherefore receive ye one another, as Christ also received us to the glory of God.
– *Romans 15:7*

JUNE 14

And he said unto them, It is not for you to know the times or the seasons, which the Father hath put in his own power. – *Acts 1:7*

JUNE 15

But ye shall receive power, after that the Holy Ghost is come upon you: and ye shall be witnesses unto me both in Jerusalem, and in all Judaea, and in Samaria, and unto the uttermost part of the earth. – *Acts 1:8*

JUNE 16

And thou shalt love the LORD thy God with all thine heart, and with all thy soul, and with all thy might. – *Deuteronomy 6:5*

JUNE 17

How beautiful upon the mountains are the feet of him that bringeth good tidings, that publisheth peace; that bringeth good tidings of good, that publisheth salvation; that saith unto Zion, Thy God reigneth! – *Isaiah 52:7*

JUNE 18
And Jesus came and spake unto them, saying, All power is given unto me in heaven and in earth. – *Matthew 28:18*

JUNE 19
Go ye therefore, and teach all nations, baptizing them in the name of the Father, and of the Son, and of the Holy Ghost. – *Matthew 28:19*

JUNE 20
Teaching them to observe all things whatsoever I have commanded you: and, lo, I am with you alway, even unto the end of the world. – *Matthew 28:20*

JUNE 21
Then saith he unto his disciples, The harvest truly is plenteous, but the labourers are few. – *Matthew 9:37*

JUNE 22
Pray ye therefore the Lord of the harvest, that he will send forth labourers into his harvest. – *Matthew 9:38*

JUNE 23
For what shall it profit a man, if he shall gain the whole world, and lose his own soul? – *Mark 8:36*

JUNE 24
A soft answer turneth away wrath: but grievous words stir up anger. – *Proverbs 15:1*

JUNE 25
And if a house be divided against itself, that house cannot stand. – *Mark 3:25*

JUNE 26
How then shall they call on him in whom they have not believed? and how shall they believe in him of whom they have not heard? and how shall they hear without a preacher?
– *Romans 10:14*

JUNE 27
Suffer the little children to come unto me, and forbid them not: for of such is the kingdom of God. – *Mark 10:14b*

JUNE 28
We love him, because he first loved us.
– *1 John 4:19*

JUNE 29
For I was an hungred, and ye gave me meat: I was thirsty, and ye gave me drink: I was a stranger, and ye took me in: Naked, and ye clothed me: I was sick, and ye visited me: I was in prison, and ye came unto me.
– *Matthew 25:35-36*

JUNE 30
These things I command you, that ye love one another. – *John 15:17*

JULY 1
Greater love hath no man than this, that a man lay down his life for his friends. – *John 15:13*

JULY 2

Then shall the righteous answer him, saying,
Lord, when saw we thee an hungred, and fed
thee? or thirsty, and gave thee drink? When
saw we thee a stranger, and took thee in? or
naked, and clothed thee? Or when saw we
thee sick, or in prison, and came unto thee?
– *Matthew 25:37-39*

JULY 3

Verily I say unto you, Inasmuch as ye have
done it unto one of the least of these my
brethren, ye have done it unto me.
– *Matthew 25:40b*

JULY 4

Jesus said unto him, Thou shalt love the Lord
thy God with all thy heart, and with all thy
soul, and with all thy mind. This is the first
and great commandment. – *Matthew 22:37-38*

JULY 5

And the second is like unto it, Thou shalt love
thy neighbour as thyself. On these two commandments hang all the law and the prophets.
– *Matthew 22:39-40*

JULY 6

Wherefore by their fruits ye shall know them.
– *Matthew 7:20*

JULY 7

Two are better than one; because they have a
good reward for their labour. – *Ecclesiastes 4:9*

JULY 8
But I say unto you, Love your enemies, bless them that curse you, do good to them that hate you, and pray for them which despitefully use you, and persecute you.
— *Matthew 5:44*

JULY 9
And Ruth said, Intreat me not to leave thee, or to return from following after thee: for whither thou goest, I will go; and where thou lodgest, I will lodge: thy people shall be my people, and thy God my God. — *Ruth 1:16*

JULY 10
Pleasant words are as an honeycomb, sweet to the soul, and health to the bones.
— *Proverbs 16:24*

JULY 11
Love not the world, neither the things that are in the world. If any man love the world, the love of the Father is not in him. — *1 John 2:15*

JULY 12
There is no fear in love; but perfect love casteth out fear: because fear hath torment. He that feareth is not made perfect in love.
— *1 John 4:18*

JULY 13
Thou wilt keep him in perfect peace, whose mind is stayed on thee: because he trusteth in thee. — *Isaiah 26:3*

JULY 14

For this is the love of God, that we keep his commandments: and his commandments are not grievous. – *1 John 5:3*

JULY 15

And whosoever shall give to drink unto one of these little ones a cup of cold water only in the name of a disciple, verily I say unto you, he shall in no wise lose his reward.
– *Matthew 10:42*

JULY 16

And the gospel must first be published among all nations. – *Mark 13:10*

JULY 17

Beloved, let us love one another: for love is of God; and every one that loveth is born of God, and knoweth God. He that loveth not knoweth not God; for God is love. – *1 John 4:7-8*

JULY 18

And walk in love, as Christ also hath loved us, and hath given himself for us an offering and a sacrifice to God for a sweetsmelling savour.
– *Ephesians 5:2*

JULY 19

And how shall they preach, except they be sent? as it is written, How beautiful are the feet of them that preach the gospel of peace, and bring glad tidings of good things!
– *Romans 10:15*

JULY 20
That at the name of Jesus every knee should bow, of things in heaven, and things in earth, and things under the earth. – *Philippians 2:10*

JULY 21
By this shall all men know that ye are my disciples, if ye have love one to another.
– *John 13:35*

JULY 22
Herein is love, not that we loved God, but that he loved us, and sent his Son to be the propitiation for our sins. – *1 John 4:10*

JULY 23
Beloved, if God so loved us, we ought also to love one another. – *1 John 4:11*

JULY 24
No man hath seen God at any time. If we love one another, God dwelleth in us, and his love is perfected in us. – *1 John 4:12*

JULY 25
Hereby know we that we dwell in him, and he in us, because he hath given us of his Spirit.
– *1 John 4:13*

JULY 26
But without faith it is impossible to please him: for he that cometh to God must believe that he is, and that he is a rewarder of them that diligently seek him. – *Hebrews 11:6*

JULY 27
I love them that love me; and those that seek me early shall find me. – *Proverbs 8:17*

JULY 28
Though I speak with the tongues of men and of angels, and have not charity, I am become as sounding brass, or a tinkling cymbal.
– *1 Corinthians 13:1*

JULY 29
And though I have the gift of prophecy, and understand all mysteries, and all knowledge; and though I have all faith, so that I could remove mountains, and have not charity, I am nothing. – *1 Corinthians 13:2*

JULY 30
And though I bestow all my goods to feed the poor, and though I give my body to be burned, and have not charity, it profiteth me nothing.
– *1 Corinthians 13:3*

JULY 31
Charity suffereth long, and is kind; charity envieth not; charity vaunteth not itself, is not puffed up, Doth not behave itself unseemly, seeketh not her own, is not easily provoked, thinketh no evil. – *1 Corinthians 13:4-5*

AUGUST 1
And now abideth faith, hope, charity, these three; but the greatest of these is charity.
– *1 Corinthians 13:13*

AUGUST 2
So then faith cometh by hearing, and hearing by the word of God. – *Romans 10:17*

AUGUST 3
Blessed is the man that trusteth in the LORD, and whose hope the LORD is. – Jeremiah 17:7

AUGUST 4
Jesus saith unto him, Thomas, because thou hast seen me, thou hast believed: blessed are they that have not seen, and yet have believed. – *John 20:29*

AUGUST 5
And Jesus said unto him, Go thy way; thy faith hath made thee whole. And immediately he received his sight, and followed Jesus in the way. – *Mark 10:52*

AUGUST 6
My son, despise not the chastening of the LORD; neither be weary of his correction.
– *Proverbs 3:11*

AUGUST 7
And his disciples came to him, and awoke him, saying, Lord, save us: we perish. And he saith unto them, Why are ye fearful, O ye of little faith? Then he arose, and rebuked the winds and the sea; and there was a great calm.
– *Matthew 8:25-26*

AUGUST 8

Jesus said unto him, If thou canst believe, all things are possible to him that believeth. And straightway the father of the child cried out, and said with tears, Lord, I believe; help thou mine unbelief. – *Mark 9:23-24*

AUGUST 9

The centurion answered and said, Lord, I am not worthy that thou shouldest come under my roof: but speak the word only, and my servant shall be healed. When Jesus heard it, he marvelled, and said to them that followed, Verily I say unto you, I have not found so great faith, no, not in Israel. – *Matthew 8:8, 10*

AUGUST 10

Trust in the LORD with all thine heart; and lean not unto thine own understanding.
– *Proverbs 3:5*

AUGUST 11

In all thy ways acknowledge him, and he shall direct thy paths. – *Proverbs 3:6*

AUGUST 12

And, behold, a woman, which was diseased . . . came behind him, and touched the hem of his garment: For she said within herself, If I may but touch his garment, I shall be whole.
– *Matthew 9:20-21*

AUGUST 13

The LORD will perfect that which concerneth
me: thy mercy, O LORD, endureth for ever:
forsake not the works of thine own hands.
– *Psalm 138:8*

AUGUST 14

Consider the lilies of the field, how they grow;
they toil not, neither do they spin: And yet I
say unto you, That even Solomon in all his
glory was not arrayed like one of these.
– *Matthew 6:28b-29*

AUGUST 15

And Jesus said unto them, I am the bread of
life: he that cometh to me shall never hunger;
and he that believeth on me shall never thirst.
– *John 6:35*

AUGUST 16

My beloved spake, and said unto me, Rise up,
my love, my fair one, and come away. For, lo,
the winter is past, the rain is over and gone;
The flowers appear on the earth; the time of
the singing of birds is come, and the voice of
the turtle is heard in our land.
– *Song of Solomon 2:10-12*

AUGUST 17

But as it is written, Eye hath not seen, nor ear
heard, neither have entered into the heart of
man, the things which God hath prepared for
them that love him. – *1 Corinthians 2:9*

AUGUST 18

Therefore take no thought, saying, What shall we eat? or, What shall we drink? or, Wherewithal shall we be clothed? . . . for your heavenly Father knoweth that ye have need of all these things. But seek ye first the kingdom of God, and his righteousness; and all these things shall be added unto you.
– *Matthew 6:31-33*

AUGUST 19

Take therefore no thought for the morrow: for the morrow shall take thought for the things of itself. Sufficient unto the day is the evil thereof. – *Matthew 6:34*

AUGUST 20

Are not two sparrows sold for a farthing? and one of them shall not fall on the ground without your Father. But the very hairs of your head are all numbered. Fear ye not therefore, ye are of more value than many sparrows.
– *Matthew 10:29-31*

AUGUST 21

Some trust in chariots, and some in horses: but we will remember the name of the LORD our God. – *Psalm 20:7*

AUGUST 22

The LORD is good, a strong hold in the day of trouble; and he knoweth them that trust in him. – *Nahum 1:7*

AUGUST 23
For I am persuaded, that neither death, nor
life, nor angels, nor principalities, nor powers,
nor things present, nor things to come, Nor
height, nor depth, nor any other creature, shall
be able to separate us from the love of God,
which is in Christ Jesus our Lord.
– *Romans 8:38-39*

AUGUST 24
Be not ye therefore like unto them: for your
Father knoweth what things ye have need of,
before ye ask him. – *Matthew 6:8*

AUGUST 25
Lay not up for yourselves treasures upon
earth, where moth and rust doth corrupt, and
where thieves break through and steal: But lay
up for yourselves treasures in heaven, where
neither moth nor rust doth corrupt, and where
thieves do not break through nor steal: For
where your treasure is, there will your heart be
also. – *Matthew 6:19-21*

AUGUST 26
He that dwelleth in the secret place of the
most High shall abide under the shadow of
the Almighty. – *Psalm 91:1*

AUGUST 27
I will say of the LORD, He is my refuge and
my fortress: my God; in him will I trust.
– *Psalm 91:2*

AUGUST 28
I am Alpha and Omega, the beginning and the end, the first and the last. – *Revelation 22:13*

AUGUST 29
Delight thyself also in the LORD; and he shall give thee the desires of thine heart. Commit thy way unto the LORD; trust also in him; and he shall bring it to pass. – *Psalm 37:4-5*

AUGUST 30
O LORD, thou hast searched me, and known me. Thou knowest my downsitting and mine uprising, thou understandest my thought afar off. – *Psalm 139:1-2*

AUGUST 31
For thou hast possessed my reins: thou hast covered me in my mother's womb. I will praise thee; for I am fearfully and wonderfully made: marvellous are thy works; and that my soul knoweth right well. – *Psalm 139:13-14*

SEPTEMBER 1
My substance was not hid from thee, when I was made in secret, and curiously wrought in the lowest parts of the earth. – *Psalm 139:15*

SEPTEMBER 2
Thine eyes did see my substance, yet being unperfect; and in thy book all my members were written, which in continuance were fashioned, when as yet there was none of them. – *Psalm 139:16*

SEPTEMBER 3
Vanity of vanities, saith the preacher; all is vanity. – *Ecclesiastes 12:8*

SEPTEMBER 4
But when thou doest alms, let not thy left hand know what thy right hand doeth: That thine alms may be in secret: and thy Father which seeth in secret himself shall reward thee openly. – *Matthew 6:3-4*

SEPTEMBER 5
But thou, when thou prayest, enter into thy closet, and when thou hast shut thy door, pray to thy Father which is in secret; and thy Father which seeth in secret shall reward thee openly. – *Matthew 6:6*

SEPTEMBER 6
Humble yourselves therefore under the mighty hand of God, that he may exalt you in due time: Casting all your care upon him; for he careth for you. – *1 Peter 5:6-7*

SEPTEMBER 7
Boast not thyself of to morrow; for thou knowest not what a day may bring forth.
– *Proverbs 27:1*

SEPTEMBER 8
Let another man praise thee, and not thine own mouth; a stranger, and not thine own lips.
– *Proverbs 27:2*

SEPTEMBER 9
The LORD seeth not as man seeth; for man looketh on the outward appearance, but the LORD looketh on the heart. – *1 Samuel 16:7b*

SEPTEMBER 10
And Jesus saith unto him, The foxes have holes, and the birds of the air have nests; but the Son of man hath not where to lay his head. – *Matthew 8:20*

SEPTEMBER 11
For whosoever exalteth himself shall be abased; and he that humbleth himself shall be exalted. – *Luke 14:11*

SEPTEMBER 12
Seek ye the LORD while he may be found, call ye upon him while he is near. – *Isaiah 55:6*

SEPTEMBER 13
And this is life eternal, that they might know thee the only true God, and Jesus Christ, whom thou hast sent. – *John 17:3*

SEPTEMBER 14
I pray for them: I pray not for the world, but for them which thou hast given me; for they are thine. – *John 17:9*

SEPTEMBER 15
Hear, O LORD, when I cry with my voice: have mercy also upon me, and answer me. – *Psalm 27:7*

SEPTEMBER 16
Confess your faults one to another, and pray one for another, that ye may be healed. The effectual fervent prayer of a righteous man availeth much. – *James 5:16*

SEPTEMBER 17
And he spake a parable unto them to this end, that men ought always to pray, and not to faint. – *Luke 18:1*

SEPTEMBER 18
Therefore I say unto you, What things soever ye desire, when ye pray, believe that ye receive them, and ye shall have them.
– *Mark 11:24*

SEPTEMBER 19
Watch and pray, that ye enter not into temptation: the spirit indeed is willing, but the flesh is weak. – *Matthew 26:41*

SEPTEMBER 20
And in that day ye shall ask me nothing. Verily, verily, I say unto you, Whatsoever ye shall ask the Father in my name, he will give it you.
– *John 16:23*

SEPTEMBER 21
O death, where is thy sting? O grave, where is thy victory? – *1 Corinthians 15:55*

SEPTEMBER 22
And all things, whatsoever ye shall ask in prayer, believing, ye shall receive.
– *Matthew 21:22*

SEPTEMBER 23
Ask, and it shall be given you; seek, and ye shall find; knock, and it shall be opened unto you. – *Matthew 7:7*

SEPTEMBER 24
For every one that asketh receiveth; and he that seeketh findeth; and to him that knocketh it shall be opened. – *Matthew 7:8*

SEPTEMBER 25
Then shall ye call upon me, and ye shall go and pray unto me, and I will hearken unto you. – *Jeremiah 29:12*

SEPTEMBER 26
And ye shall seek me, and find me, when ye shall search for me with all your heart.
– *Jeremiah 29:13*

SEPTEMBER 27
Peace I leave with you, my peace I give unto you: not as the world giveth, give I unto you. Let not your heart be troubled, neither let it be afraid. – *John 14:27*

SEPTEMBER 28
Again I say unto you, That if two of you shall agree on earth as touching any thing that they shall ask, it shall be done for them of my Father which is in heaven. – *Matthew 18:19*

SEPTEMBER 29
For where two or three are gathered together in my name, there am I in the midst of them. – *Matthew 18:20*

SEPTEMBER 30
God be merciful unto us, and bless us; and cause his face to shine upon us. – *Psalm 67:1*

OCTOBER 1
Be ye therefore merciful, as your Father also is merciful. – *Luke 6:36*

OCTOBER 2
Be ye angry, and sin not: let not the sun go down upon your wrath. – *Ephesians 4:26*

OCTOBER 3
Therefore we are buried with him by baptism into death: that like as Christ was raised up from the dead by the glory of the Father, even so we also should walk in newness of life. – *Romans 6:4*

OCTOBER 4
And when ye stand praying, forgive, if ye have aught against any: that your Father also which is in heaven may forgive you your trespasses. – *Mark 11:25*

OCTOBER 5
Judge not, and ye shall not be judged: condemn not, and ye shall not be condemned: forgive, and ye shall be forgiven. – *Luke 6:37*

OCTOBER 6
If we confess our sins, he is faithful and just to forgive us our sins, and to cleanse us from all unrighteousness. – *1 John 1:9*

OCTOBER 7
Come now, and let us reason together, saith the LORD: though your sins be as scarlet, they shall be as white as snow; though they be red like crimson, they shall be as wool.
– *Isaiah 1:18*

OCTOBER 8
Wherefore I say unto you, All manner of sin and blasphemy shall be forgiven unto men: but the blasphemy against the Holy Ghost shall not be forgiven unto men.
– *Matthew 12:31*

OCTOBER 9
A wise son maketh a glad father: but a foolish son is the heaviness of his mother.
– *Proverbs 10:1b*

OCTOBER 10
Therefore if any man be in Christ, he is a new creature: old things are passed away; behold, all things are become new. – *2 Corinthians 5:17*

OCTOBER 11

Bless the LORD, O my soul, and forget not all his benefits: Who forgiveth all thine iniquities; who healeth all thy diseases; Who redeemeth thy life from destruction; who crowneth thee with lovingkindness and tender mercies. – *Psalm 103:2-4*

OCTOBER 12

I indeed baptize you with water unto repentance: but he that cometh after me is mightier than I, whose shoes I am not worthy to bear: he shall baptize you with the Holy Ghost, and with fire. – *Matthew 3:11*

OCTOBER 13

Forbearing one another, and forgiving one another, if any man have a quarrel against any: even as Christ forgave you, so also do ye.
– *Colossians 3:13*

OCTOBER 14

The fear of the LORD is the beginning of knowledge: but fools despise wisdom and instruction. – *Proverbs 1:7*

OCTOBER 15

Teach me thy way, O LORD. – *Psalm 27:11a*

OCTOBER 16

Ye are of God, little children, and have overcome them: because greater is he that is in you, than he that is in the world. – *1 John 4:4*

OCTOBER 17
Thy word is a lamp unto my feet, and a light unto my path. – *Psalm 119:105*

OCTOBER 18
Then came Peter to him, and said, Lord, how oft shall my brother sin against me, and I forgive him? till seven times? Jesus saith unto him, I say not unto thee, Until seven times: but, Until seventy times seven.
– *Matthew 18:21-22*

OCTOBER 19
And the peace of God, which passeth all understanding, shall keep your hearts and minds through Christ Jesus. –*Philippians 4:7*

OCTOBER 20
Thy word have I hid in mine heart, that I might not sin against thee. – *Psalm 119:11*

OCTOBER 21
The fool hath said in his heart, There is no God. – *Psalm 14:1a*

OCTOBER 22
Train up a child in the way he should go: and when he is old, he will not depart from it.
– *Proverbs 22:6*

OCTOBER 23
And that every tongue should confess that Jesus Christ is Lord, to the glory of God the Father. – *Philippians 2:11*

OCTOBER 24

My son, keep thy father's commandment, and forsake not the law of thy mother.
– *Proverbs 6:20*

OCTOBER 25

For the commandment is a lamp; and the law is light; and reproofs of instruction are the way of life. – *Proverbs 6:23*

OCTOBER 26

A wise man will hear, and will increase learning; and a man of understanding shall attain unto wise counsels. – *Proverbs 1:5*

OCTOBER 27

Where there is no vision, the people perish: but he that keepeth the law, happy is he.
– *Proverbs 29:18*

OCTOBER 28

Give instruction to a wise man, and he will be yet wiser: teach a just man, and he will increase in learning. – *Proverbs 9:9*

OCTOBER 29

And that from a child thou hast known the holy scriptures, which are able to make thee wise unto salvation through faith which is in Christ Jesus. – *2 Timothy 3:15*

OCTOBER 30

All scripture is given by inspiration of God, and is profitable for doctrine, for reproof, for correction, for instruction in righteousness.
– 2 Timothy 3:16

OCTOBER 31

Again, the kingdom of heaven is like unto a merchant man, seeking goodly pearls: Who, when he had found one pearl of great price, went and sold all that he had, and bought it.
– Matthew 13:45-46

NOVEMBER 1

No man can serve two masters: for either he will hate the one, and love the other; or else he will hold to the one, and despise the other. Ye cannot serve God and mammon.
– Matthew 6:24

NOVEMBER 2

For the earth shall be filled with the knowledge of the glory of the LORD, as the waters cover the sea. *– Habakkuk 2:14*

NOVEMBER 3

Remember now thy Creator in the days of thy youth, while the evil days come not, nor the years draw nigh, when thou shalt say, I have no pleasure in them. *– Ecclesiastes 12:1*

NOVEMBER 4
Whoso loveth instruction loveth knowledge: but he that hateth reproof is brutish.
– *Proverbs 12:1*

NOVEMBER 5
Be not deceived; God is not mocked: for whatsoever a man soweth, that shall he also reap.
– *Galatians 6:7*

NOVEMBER 6
If any of you lack wisdom, let him ask of God, that giveth to all men liberally, and upbraideth not; and it shall be given him. – *James 1:5*

NOVEMBER 7
Search the scriptures; for in them ye think ye have eternal life: and they are they which testify of me. – *John 5:39*

NOVEMBER 8
Incline thine ear unto wisdom, and apply thine heart to understanding. – *Proverbs 2:2*

NOVEMBER 9
A good name is rather to be chosen than great riches, and loving favour rather than silver and gold. – *Proverbs 22:1*

NOVEMBER 10
There is no peace, saith the LORD, unto the wicked. – *Isaiah 48:22*

NOVEMBER 11
Because that, when they knew God, they glorified him not as God, neither were thankful; but became vain in their imaginations, and their foolish heart was darkened. Professing themselves to be wise, they became fools.
– *Romans 1:21-22*

NOVEMBER 12
And whosoever shall not receive you, nor hear your words, when ye depart out of that house or city, shake off the dust of your feet.
– *Matthew 10:14*

NOVEMBER 13
But the wisdom that is from above is first pure, then peaceable, gentle, and easy to be entreated, full of mercy and good fruits, without partiality, and without hypocrisy.
– *James 3:17*

NOVEMBER 14
And the fruit of righteousness is sown in peace of them that make peace. – *James 3:18*

NOVEMBER 15
And the rain descended, and the floods came, and the winds blew, and beat upon that house; and it fell not: for it was founded upon a rock.
– *Matthew 7:25*

NOVEMBER 16
He that believeth on the Son hath everlasting life: and he that believeth not the Son shall not see life; but the wrath of God abideth on him. – *John 3:36*

NOVEMBER 17
Therefore being justified by faith, we have peace with God through our Lord Jesus Christ. – *Romans 5:1*

NOVEMBER 18
But God commendeth his love toward us, in that, while we were yet sinners, Christ died for us. – *Romans 5:8*

NOVEMBER 19
Then Jesus beholding him loved him, and said unto him, One thing thou lackest: go thy way, sell whatsoever thou hast, and give to the poor, and thou shalt have treasure in heaven: and come, take up the cross, and follow me. – *Mark 10:21*

NOVEMBER 20
But whosoever drinketh of the water that I shall give him shall never thirst; but the water that I shall give him shall be in him a well of water springing up into everlasting life. – *John 4:14*

NOVEMBER 21

For he shall grow up before him as a tender plant, and as a root out of a dry ground: he hath no form nor comeliness; and when we shall see him, there is no beauty that we should desire him. – *Isaiah 53:2*

NOVEMBER 22

He is despised and rejected of men; a man of sorrows, and acquainted with grief: and we hid as it were our faces from him; he was despised, and we esteemed him not. – *Isaiah 53:3*

NOVEMBER 23

But he was wounded for our transgressions, he was bruised for our iniquities: the chastisement of our peace was upon him; and with his stripes we are healed. – *Isaiah 53:5*

NOVEMBER 24

All we like sheep have gone astray; we have turned every one to his own way; and the LORD hath laid on him the iniquity of us all. – *Isaiah 53:6*

NOVEMBER 25

That if thou shalt confess with thy mouth the Lord Jesus, and shalt believe in thine heart that God hath raised him from the dead, thou shalt be saved. – *Romans 10:9*

NOVEMBER 26

For with the heart man believeth unto right-eousness; and with the mouth confession is made unto salvation. For the scripture saith, Whosoever believeth on him shall not be ashamed. – *Romans 10:10-11*

NOVEMBER 27

Except ye be converted, and become as little children, ye shall not enter into the kingdom of heaven. – *Matthew 18:3b*

NOVEMBER 28

For all have sinned, and come short of the glory of God. – *Romans 3:23*

NOVEMBER 29

Being justified freely by his grace through the redemption that is in Christ Jesus: Whom God hath set forth to be a propitiation through faith in his blood, to declare his righteousness for the remission of sins that are past, through the forbearance of God. – *Romans 3:24-25*

NOVEMBER 30

I am the door: by me if any man enter in, he shall be saved, and shall go in and out, and find pasture. – *John 10:9*

DECEMBER 1

I am come that they might have life, and that they might have it more abundantly.
– *John 10:10b*

DECEMBER 2
I am the good shepherd: the good shepherd giveth his life for the sheep. – *John 10:11*

DECEMBER 3
But as many as received him, to them gave he power to become the sons of God, even to them that believe on his name. – *John 1:12*

DECEMBER 4
Neither is there salvation in any other: for there is none other name under heaven given among men, whereby we must be saved.
– *Acts 4:12*

DECEMBER 5
For the wages of sin is death; but the gift of God is eternal life through Jesus Christ our Lord. – *Romans 6:23*

DECEMBER 6
Jesus saith unto him, I am the way, the truth, and the life: no man cometh unto the Father, but by me. – *John 14:6*

DECEMBER 7
And they said, Believe on the Lord Jesus Christ, and thou shalt be saved, and thy house. – *Acts 16:31*

DECEMBER 8
He is not here: for he is risen, as he said. Come, see the place where the Lord lay.
– *Matthew 28:6*

DECEMBER 9

No man knoweth the Son, but the Father; neither knoweth any man the Father, save the Son, and he to whomsoever the Son will reveal him. – *Matthew 11:27b*

DECEMBER 10

Christ died for our sins according to the scriptures; And that he was buried, and that he rose again the third day according to the scriptures. – *1 Corinthians 15:3b-4*

DECEMBER 11

For he hath made him to be sin for us, who knew no sin; that we might be made the righteousness of God in him. – *2 Corinthians 5:21*

DECEMBER 12

For God so loved the world, that he gave his only begotten Son, that whosoever believeth in him should not perish, but have everlasting life. – *John 3:16*

DECEMBER 13

For God sent not his Son into the world to condemn the world; but that the world through him might be saved. – *John 3:17*

DECEMBER 14

For I know that my redeemer liveth, and that he shall stand at the latter day upon the earth. – *Job 19:25*

DECEMBER 15
There is one body, and one Spirit, even as ye
are called in one hope of your calling.
– *Ephesians 4:4*

DECEMBER 16
One Lord, one faith, one baptism.
– *Ephesians 4:5*

DECEMBER 17
One God and Father of all, who is above all,
and through all, and in you all. – *Ephesians 4:6*

DECEMBER 18
But unto every one of us is given grace accord-
ing to the measure of the gift of Christ.
– *Ephesians 4:7*

DECEMBER 19
Blessed be the Lord God of Israel; for he hath
visited and redeemed his people. – *Luke 1:68*

DECEMBER 20
The grass withereth, the flower fadeth: but
the word of our God shall stand for ever.
– *Isaiah 40:8*

DECEMBER 21
When the Son of man shall come in his glory,
and all the holy angels with him, then shall he
sit upon the throne of his glory.
– *Matthew 25:31*

DECEMBER 22

For as many as are led by the Spirit of God, they are the sons of God. – *Romans 8:14*

DECEMBER 23

And Simon Peter answered and said, Thou art the Christ, the Son of the living God.
– *Matthew 16:16*

DECEMBER 24

And I say also unto thee, That thou art Peter, and upon this rock I will build my church; and the gates of hell shall not prevail against it.
– *Matthew 16:18*

DECEMBER 25

And the angel said unto them, Fear not: for, behold, I bring you good tidings of great joy, which shall be to all people. For unto you is born this day in the city of David a Saviour, which is Christ the Lord. – *Luke 2:10-11*

DECEMBER 26

The heavens shall vanish away like smoke, and the earth shall wax old like a garment, and they that dwell therein shall die in like manner: but my salvation shall be for ever, and my righteousness shall not be abolished.
– *Isaiah 51:6b*

DECEMBER 27

In the beginning was the Word, and the Word was with God, and the Word was God.
– *John 1:1*

DECEMBER 28
Behold, I shew you a mystery; We shall not all sleep, but we shall all be changed.
– *1 Corinthians 15:51*

DECEMBER 29
In a moment, in the twinkling of an eye, at the last trump: for the trumpet shall sound, and the dead shall be raised incorruptible, and we shall be changed. – *1 Corinthians 15:52*

DECEMBER 30
For this corruptible must put on incorruption, and this mortal must put on immortality.
– *1 Corinthians 15:53*

DECEMBER 31
So when this corruptible shall have put on incorruption, and this mortal shall have put on immortality, then shall be brought to pass the saying that is written, Death is swallowed up in victory. – *1 Corinthians 15:54*

PRAYER LIST

PRAYER LIST

63

PRAYER LIST

_____

_____

_____

_____

_____

_____

_____

_____

_____

_____

_____

_____

_____

_____

_____

_____

_____

_____

_____

_____

_____

_____

_____